spitting cobra

POISONOUS SNAKES

SEYMOUR SIMON

ILLUSTRATIONS BY
WILLIAM R. DOWNEY

DOVER PUBLICATIONS, INC.
MINEOLA, NEW YORK

Copyright

Bibliographical Note

Poisonous Snakes, first published by Dover Publications, Inc., in 2012, is an unabridged republication of the work originally published by Four Winds Press, New York, in 1981.

Library of Congress Cataloging-in-Publication Data

Simon, Seymour.
    Poisonous snakes / Seymour Simon ; [illustrated by] William Downey.
      p. cm.
    "Poisonous Snakes, first published by Dover Publications, Inc., in 2012, is an unabridged republication of the work originally published by Four Winds Press, New York, in 1981"—T.p. verso.
    Summary: "There are more than 250 kinds of poisonous snakes, and this illustrated book tells where they live, what they eat, and how they behave. You'll also find out which snakes pose no danger to humans, how snakes are "milked," how anti-venom is made, and what to do if you're bitten. 26 illustrations"— Provided by publisher.
    ISBN-13: 978-0-486-48470-9 (pbk.)
    ISBN-10: 0-486-48470-X (pbk.)
    1. Poisonous snakes—Juvenile literature. I. Downey, William, 1954– ill. II. Title.

QL666.06S4554 2012
597.96—dc23
                                      2011036107

Manufactured in the United States by Courier Corporation
48470X01
www.doverpublications.com

CONTENTS

There are many stories of attacks on people by poisonous snakes. One such story out of Africa tells of the dreaded black mamba, one of the most dangerous snakes in the world.

It seems that two children were out for a ride on their horses one day. The horses accidentally trotted near a pair of black mambas. When they saw the snakes, the children galloped away at full speed. The mambas gave chase. The children urged their horses to go even faster.

It was no use. The angry snakes swiftly overtook the speeding horses. They leaped up and bit the youngsters on their

black mamba

necks. Then the snakes bit the horses. In a few minutes, the poison took effect. Both the youngsters and their horses were dead.

It's a dreadful story. The black mamba is very fast and active for a snake. It is more likely than any other snake to deliberately attack a person. In addition, the black mamba is very poisonous and its bite usually causes death.

But this story could not possibly be true. There is no snake in the world that could catch a horse at full gallop. In fact, an able-bodied person can outrun any snake with ease. It is also very unlikely that any snake will go after a human being more than a few feet away.

It is a fact that some poisonous snakes will attack a nearby person. Usually it's because the person comes upon the snake suddenly and disturbs it. The snake may strike out because it is startled.

At other times a snake will bite a person because it is cornered. The person may be standing between the snake and its usual shelter. The snake will strike in an attempt to escape.

But most of the time poisonous snakes will not attack people who come too near. They usually remain completely still and are often overlooked. Or they quickly crawl away.

What are some true stories about the way poisonous snakes behave? Which snakes are the most dangerous? Where do poisonous snakes live? Do you have to worry about being bitten? What does poison do to a person? What should you do if you're bitten by a snake you think may be poisonous? In this book we'll look at the answers to these and other questions you may have about poisonous snakes.

Some people think that all snakes are poisonous. In fact, most snakes are quite harmless. There are about twenty-five hundred different kinds of snakes in the world. Only about two hundred fifty of these are poisonous. And only a little more than half of these are really dangerous to humans.

However, the dangerous kinds live almost everywhere that people live. Except for some islands, such as Ireland and Hawaii, the snowfields of the polar regions, and high mountains, poisonous snakes live in all parts of the world. Almost every state in the United States has poisonous snakes. In Arizona alone there are seventeen different kinds of rattlesnakes.

Poisonous snakes don't all look the same. There is no way that you can tell a poisonous snake from a harmless one just by looking at its body or head shape. Some people think that all poisonous snakes have a heavy, triangular head and small, narrow eyes. They think that harmless snakes are thinner with big, round eyes.

saw-scaled
viper

puff adder

In the United States, most kinds of poisonous snakes do have a heavy, triangular head and narrow eyes. They look like the popular idea of a poisonous snake. But that is not so in Africa and Asia. Some of the world's deadliest snakes are slender with small heads and large eyes.

Also, some nonpoisonous snakes look very much like poisonous ones. For example, the harmless hog-nosed snake has a heavy body and head. If a hog-nosed snake is threatened, it flattens its neck and seems about to strike. It also hisses as if in warning. For that reason, the hog-nosed snake is often mistakenly called a puff adder.

Yet the hog-nosed snake will almost never bite a person, even if it is attacked. In fact, if a hog-nosed snake is attacked, it will flop over on its back and look as if it is dead. Probably many harmless snakes are killed by people who mistake them for poisonous snakes.

There are other poisonous and nonpoisonous snakes that look almost alike. For example, North American coral snakes have red, yellow, and black rings banding their whole bodies. These short, slender snakes are related to cobras and their venom is very dangerous to humans. The scarlet king snake is about the same size and shape. It, too, is banded with rings

hog-nosed snake

of red, yellow, and black. It looks much like the coral snake, but it is completely nonpoisonous and quite harmless.

Poisonous snakes are a much greater problem in some parts of the world than in others. Europe has only a few poisonous snakes, and most of them are not very large or dangerous. England has only a single kind of poisonous snake and Ireland has none at all. The United States, Canada, and Europe have poisonous snakes, but few reported deaths from them. In India, Mexico, Brazil, and parts of southeast Asia and Africa, poisonous snakes claim many victims each year. In these places, snakebite is an important health problem.

In the United States and Canada, there are only about one dozen cases of fatal snakebite each year. In Mexico, with many people living in the countryside and many poisonous snakes, the number of cases is about ten times greater than in the United States and Canada combined. But no place in the world even comes close to matching India for the number of deaths from snakebite. Each year, anywhere from fifteen thousand to twenty thousand Indians die of snakebite. That's one half of all reported deaths from snakebite in the world.

It is easy to see why the problem is so great. Eighty different kinds of poisonous snakes are found in India, including at least a dozen that are highly dangerous. India is an overcrowded country, with many people living in the countryside far from medical attention.

It is impossible to know exactly how many people die of snakebite in the world each year. Many of the people who are bitten live in areas where few records are kept. Some scientists think that each year more than thirty thousand people are killed by poisonous snakes.

Poisonous snakes have glands in their heads which produce a special kind of saliva called venom. Venom can cause illness and death in other animals when it is injected into their blood. Nonpoisonous snakes have similar glands in their heads, but these produce ordinary saliva.

A poisonous snake uses its venom when hunting other animals for food. For example, rattlesnakes feed on small animals such as rabbits, rats, and lizards. When a small animal is bitten, the effect is almost immediate. The victim may hop a few times and kick with its legs. In a minute or two, the animal is helpless. In another few minutes, it is dead.

No one is sure why some animals but not others are harmed by a particular snake's venom. For example, mammals are quickly affected by rattlesnake venom, but other snakes are not. On the other hand, coral snakes' venom is deadly to other snakes and to mammals as well.

Different snakes produce different kinds of venom. Most cobras and their relatives produce a venom that affects the nerves of an animal. The muscles of the victim are paralyzed, and it cannot move. If the venom reaches the muscles around the lungs, the animal will suffocate and die.

Viper venoms and most rattlesnake venoms usually work in a different way. The venom enters the bloodstream and destroys the blood cells and surrounding tissues.

There are some snakes, such as Russell's viper and some cobras, whose venom is of both types. This makes these snakes even more deadly.

Curiously, snake venom usually must get into the bloodstream of an animal to have much effect. Experimenters have fed laboratory rats large amounts of rattlesnake venom without causing any ill effects. But the same amount of venom injected into the bloodstream would have killed dozens of the rats.

Venom is injected by a snake's fangs, which are a special kind of teeth found only in the upper jaws of poisonous snakes.

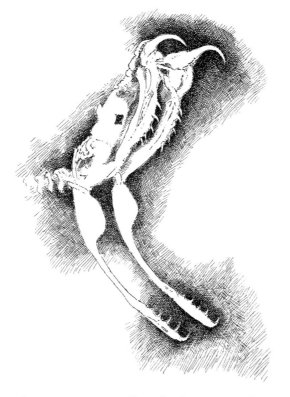

A snake's ordinary teeth are solid and curved backward. They are pointed and useful for grabbing prey, but not for chewing. Prey is always swallowed whole.

The fangs of most poisonous snakes are not solid, but have a hollow channel inside. The channel has an opening at the upper end to receive the venom from the snake's poison glands. At the lower end, there is a smaller hole just above the pointed tip through which the venom is injected into the prey. The hypodermic needle was modeled after the fang of a poisonous snake.

snake fangs

12

Fangs are shed from time to time. Behind each fang there are several replacement fangs in different stages of growth. When a fang is about to drop out, a replacement slowly moves forward into place in a nearby socket.

For a few days there are two fangs on one side of the mouth. Then the old fang drops out or is left stuck in the prey after a bite. In this way there is always at least one usable fang on each side of a snake's mouth. As the snake grows larger with age, so, too, does the size of the replacement fangs.

Dr. Vital Brazil, a Brazilian scientist, was one of the first people to use the venom of poisonous snakes to produce a medicine for snakebite. Starting in 1899, he kept hundreds of deadly snakes in cages on a snake farm.

Nowadays there are snake farms in many parts of the world. The snakes are "milked" of their venom every few days. "Milking" a poisonous snake is a dangerous job. A person grabs the snake firmly just behind its head. Then a small bottle with a gauze covering is brought toward the snake. The snake bites the gauze and a few drops of venom fall into the bottle.

milking

The venom is then treated and weakened. The weak venom is injected into a horse or other large animal. Over a period of time the animal develops substances in its blood called antivenins, which counteract the venom. The antivenins are then removed from the animal's blood and stored for use with human snakebite victims.

Each kind of poisonous snake kept on the farm is used to make a different antivenin. Today there are antivenins available for all of the world's poisonous snakes. They have been responsible for saving thousands of human lives.

Scientists have classed most poisonous snakes into four main groups. The first of the major groups includes the cobras and their relatives, such as the mambas and the coral snakes. A second group is made up of poisonous sea snakes. A third group is the true vipers. The fourth group is the pit vipers, which includes the many kinds of rattlesnakes.

The cobras of Africa and Asia, the mambas of Africa, the coral snakes of America, and all the poisonous snakes of Australia are known as *elapid* snakes. All of the elapids are front-fanged snakes. These snakes have their poison fangs rigidly fixed in their upper front jaws. The fangs are always erect and ready for use.

Most of the elapids have a venom which attacks the nervous system. The family of elapids includes some of the largest and most dangerous snakes in the world.

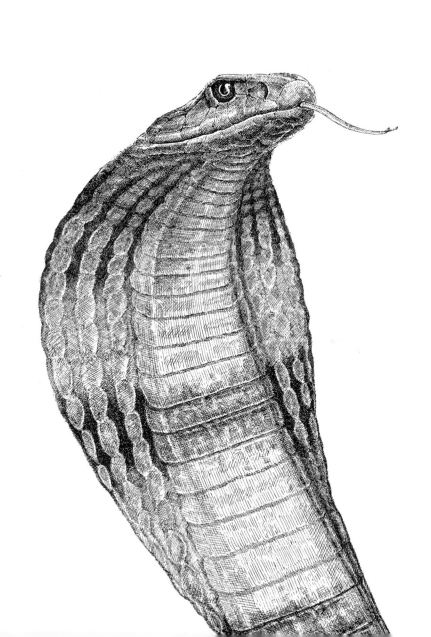

Cobras

The *king cobra* is the largest poisonous snake in the world. Adults often reach a length of fourteen feet. The largest king cobra on record was measured at more than eighteen feet. Because of its great size and aggressiveness, the king cobra presents a real danger to large animals and humans. Many experts think that the king cobra is the most dangerous snake in the world. Its venom is powerful enough to kill even an elephant, and there are reports of that actually happening.

A large king cobra can raise its head five or six feet off the

king cobra ground before it strikes. It is particularly likely to bite during its mating season. But the king cobra is unpredictable. It may just as readily move away when a person comes near.

The king cobra is the only cobra that builds a nest. It is made of leaves and branches. The female lays twenty to forty eggs and guards them until they hatch. The male often stays nearby. When the eggs hatch, the young cobras are about twenty inches long.

The scientific name for the king cobra, *Ophiophagus,* means "snake-eater." The name fits because the king cobra eats mostly snakes, both poisonous and nonpoisonous ones. Once in a while it will also eat a lizard or a small mammal or bird.

The king cobra is found throughout southeast Asia, India, southern China, and some nearby islands. Despite its large range, it is not a very common snake. It lives on the ground, but can also climb trees and swim in water.

Adult king cobras are brown or olive gray. Some have lighter bands of color across their bodies. Their hoods are narrow and unmarked.

The *Indian cobra* is also known as the spectacled cobra, because of eyelike markings on its hood. Early Portuguese sailors who visited India had still another name for this snake. They called it the snake of the hood. The name became so well known that any snake with a hood was called a cobra.

But of all the hooded snakes, few can spread their hoods as much as the Indian cobra. It does this by raising and pushing forward the long ribs behind its neck. The skin stretches across the ribs, forming a flat surface that may be four times as wide as the snake's body.

Snake charmers usually use the Indian cobra in their acts. The snake charmer begins to play a tune and sways back and forth in front of a large basket. Slowly the snake rises up until a third of its body is in the air. Its hood enlarges and flattens out. It often hisses as if in warning.

Actually, all snakes are deaf and the cobra is responding to the sight of a person in front of it rather than to the music. Sometimes the cobras in these acts have had their poison

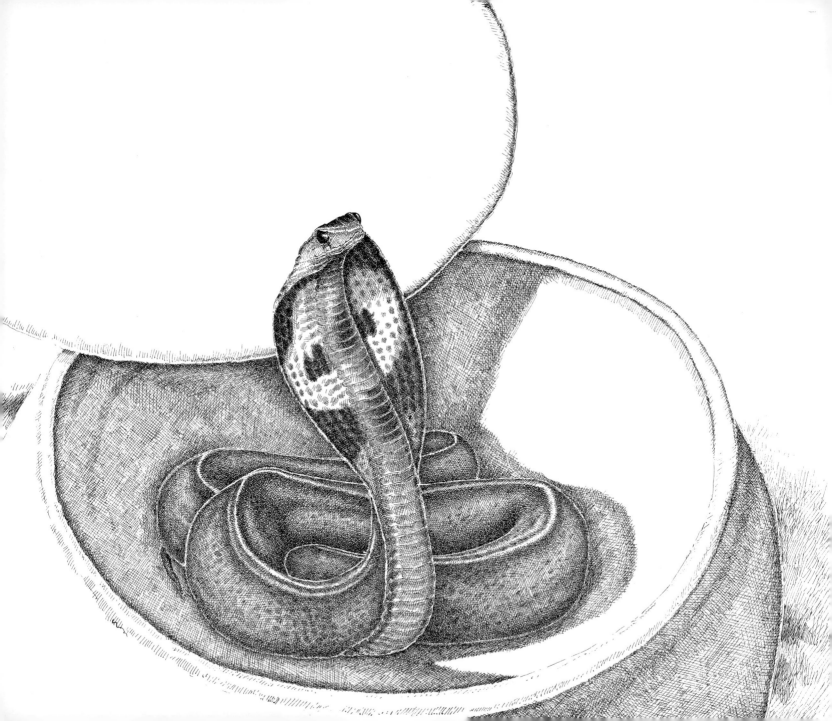

fangs removed; they are harmless. But that is not always so. Some snake charmers accidentally have been bitten and a few have died as a result.

The Indian cobra is not a very large snake, only about one third the size of the king cobra. It lives in almost any type of country from wooded areas to open plains. It ranges all over India, southeast Asia, and the Philippine Islands. Because it is commonly found in populated areas, the Indian cobra is far more likely than the rarer king cobra to bite a person.

Two African cobras, the *ringhals* and the *black-necked cobra,* are known as spitting cobras. These cobras are small, usually only about three or four feet long. They don't often bite humans, but they can still be quite dangerous.

The poison tubes in the fangs of these cobras turn outward near the tip. If a large animal or a person comes too near one of these snakes, it rises up and opens its mouth. Then it squirts a jet of venom through its fangs a distance of six to ten feet. The venom seems to be aimed at the eyes of the animal or

Indian cobra person.

The venom that hits the eyes of a person is not usually enough to kill, but it does cause severe pain and sometimes even blindness. These cobras can spit their venom between a dozen and twenty times, one jet right after another.

The ringhals cobra has still another dangerous trick. When a large animal comes near, the ringhals may pretend that it is dead. It turns its head upside down and lets its mouth hang open. But if the ringhals is touched, it will suddenly bite or squirt venom at its attacker.

Mambas

Mambas are found only in Africa. The *black mamba* is the largest African poisonous snake and the most feared. An average-sized adult is ten feet long, but some are longer than fourteen feet. The black mamba is a slender, fast-moving snake. It strikes quickly and has a deadly nerve venom.

The black mamba has large fangs which are located very far forward. It often stays hidden from view among rocks or long grasses. It is easy for a person to come upon a mamba accidentally. That's one more reason why the snake is so dangerous.

The *green mamba* is about half the size of the black mamba. The green mamba spends much of its life in trees. Its green

color makes it difficult to spot against a background of leaves. The green mamba preys upon birds and lizards that live in trees. It grips its prey with its poisonous upper fangs and also with large teeth in its lower jaw.

The green mamba is much less dangerous to people than the black mamba is. The green mamba will usually move away and avoid any large animal. But it does have a dangerous bite and can cause death.

The green mamba is sometimes confused with another poisonous African snake called the *boomslang*. They are both slim snakes that live in trees. The boomslang is not a member of the elapid family. It is one of the very few poisonous snakes that are rear-fanged. It has three large fangs in each upper jaw in back of several solid front teeth. But the fangs are close enough to the front of the mouth to be easily used in biting prey. The boomslang is not an especially dangerous snake. It will usually flee from a person rather than attack.

green mamba

Coral Snakes

All of the different kinds of coral snakes live in North and South America. The *common coral snake* is usually about two feet long. It is a pretty snake, with bands of red, yellow, and black over its entire body. Like the other elapids, the common coral snake is front-fanged and highly venomous. But its teeth are small and it rarely bites humans. When it does bite, however, its venom usually causes death.

Different kinds of coral snakes are found in Mexico and South and Central America. Most—but not all—are banded with red, yellow, and black. They usually burrow in the ground and are not often seen. Their main foods are snakes and lizards.

coral snake

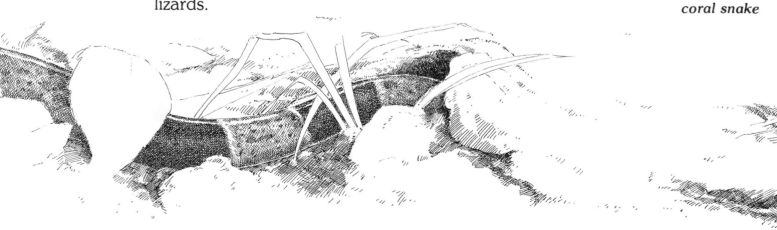

Australian Snakes

Australia is the only continent where poisonous snakes outnumber the nonpoisonous kinds. There are more than eighty-five different kinds of poisonous snakes that make their homes in Australia. One of the most dangerous is the *death adder*. The death adder is not really an adder (viper) at all, but a member of the elapid family.

The death adder is usually only about three feet long. It has a wide body, flattened head, and a short tail that comes to a tip. Its color varies and often matches its surroundings. It usually stays still, waiting for prey to come near. Sometimes the death adder waves its tail in front of its head as a lure to attract the lizards on which it feeds.

If a death adder is accidentally stepped upon, its bite can be very dangerous. According to some scientists, about 50

taipan

percent of the people bitten by a death adder will die. Some people who live in Australia think that the death adder can sting with its tail, but this is not so.

The *tiger snake* gets its name from the tigerlike yellow stripes that cover its body. It is a common snake in eastern and southern Australia and very poisonous. It has very large numbers of young, up to fifty in one litter. The death rate from its bite is about 40 percent, making it a very dangerous animal.

The *taipan* is one of the most deadly snakes in the world. It is a large snake that grows to more than ten feet. When it bites, it injects an enormous amount of highly poisonous nerve venom. A person bitten by this snake will probably die within a few minutes. The only reason that the taipan doesn't kill more people is that it lives in very lightly populated areas of northeast Australia. It is rarely seen because it is scarce and will usually try to escape rather than attack.

All of the fifty different kinds of sea snakes are poisonous. Their poisonous fangs and venom are much like those of the cobras and other elapids. The fangs are hollow, permanently erect, and located in the front of the mouth. The venom glands of a sea snake are located just below the eyes.

Most sea snakes live in the warmer coastal waters of the western Pacific and Indian oceans. Most kinds are between four and six feet long. Even the largest are only about eight to ten feet long. They feed entirely on fish, which they hunt at any hour of the day or night.

Most sea snakes have very powerful venom. One kind of sea snake has venom that is fifty times more poisonous than that of the king cobra. When a fish is bitten by a sea snake, it stiffens and dies within seconds.

All sea snakes are excellent swimmers. They have flattened, paddle-shaped tails which they use to propel themselves through the water. A few kinds come ashore to lay eggs. But most never come out onto dry land. They give birth to living young at sea.

On land, most sea snakes are almost helpless. They do not have the large flat scales found on the undersides of other snakes, and so they can't get a grip on the ground. They will flop around and squirm, almost unable to crawl.

A sea snake will drown if held underwater for too long. It must come to the surface to breathe air. When a sea snake is underwater, it closes its nostrils with a small flap or valve. When it comes up for air, it keeps its head partly submerged while the valves open to allow it to breathe.

The sea snake has a large single lung which stretches practically the whole length of its body. The back part of the lung seems to act like a kind of float and also stores air for use in dives.

black-and-yellow sea snake

Some kinds of sea snakes bask in the sunlight on the surface of the water. They will usually dive and disappear when a boat approaches. People have reported seeing huge numbers of sea snakes on certain days. One such report appeared in 1932 in the book *The Trail That Is Always New,* by W. Low. It describes a solid mass of sea snakes squirming on the surface near the island of Sumatra. The mass was described as *ten feet wide and sixty miles long!* There must have been millions of snakes to make up a mass that large.

Sea snakes are attracted by lights at night. Native fishermen hold lanterns over the water when they fish at night. Sometimes sea snakes get entangled in their nets. The fishermen unravel the snakes from the nets and throw them out by hand. It seems dangerous, yet few of the men are bitten. It seems that a sea snake will very rarely bite a person. Bathers, for example, are never attacked by sea snakes.

Even so, they do pose some danger. The United States Navy rates sea snakes as a three-plus danger, on a scale of one plus (minimum) to four plus (maximum). They suggest that it would be best for divers to leave the water when sea snakes are around, especially when they are breeding. And, of course, sea snakes should never be captured or touched by anybody who isn't an expert in poisonous snakes.

The *black-banded sea snake* is found from the Bay of Bengal to Japan and Australia. It lays eggs on land and is one of the few kinds of sea snakes that can move fairly well out of the water. It lives in coastal waters, coral reefs, river mouths, and harbors. It is a small snake, about three to four feet long.

Of all the sea snakes, the *black-and-yellow sea snake* is the one best adapted to life in the water. It is a fast swimmer and never leaves the water. It gives birth to living young at sea. Adults grow to three or four feet in length. This wanderer has been found all over the Pacific from west to east. It has even been found as far north as Siberian waters. It is the only sea snake to travel far into deep waters.

Vipers have the most highly developed venom glands and fangs of all the poisonous snakes. All of the vipers have poison fangs in the front of the upper jaw. But their fangs are not fixed in place as they are in the cobra family. When not in use, the viper's fangs lie folded back along a sort of pocket in the upper jaw. When the viper is about to bite, the fangs spring forward and are ready for use.

The fangs of most vipers are longer and more curved than those of cobras. Often the fangs are so long that it is impossible for vipers to close their mouths when their fangs are erect.

Vipers have large venom glands in their heads which are connected by ducts to the fangs. The large venom glands take up the space in their heavy, triangular heads. Most vipers are short, heavy-bodied snakes.

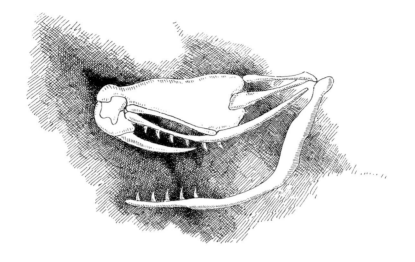

viper fangs

Rather than moving after prey, most vipers often lie in wait for small animals. When an animal comes within striking distance, the viper is ready.

Before a viper strikes, it tilts its head backward. Its lower jaw drops and the long fangs in the upper jaw sweep outward. With its mouth open to the widest possible angle, the fangs point straight forward.

At the same time that the viper opens its mouth, its head launches forward, driving the fangs into the body of its prey. As the fangs dig in, muscles in the snake's head squeeze the venom glands. The venom is pushed through the ducts and the fangs into the victim.

Vipers usually don't hang on to their prey. The first bite injects enough venom. The bitten animal may move away, but it will die after a few minutes. The viper trails the animal until it dies, and then eats it.

The viper family is made up of two large subfamilies: true vipers and pit vipers. The true vipers are found mostly in Africa, with a few kinds in Europe and Asia. The pit vipers, the subfamily which includes rattlesnakes, live mostly in the Americas.

The *Gaboon viper* has unbelievably long fangs. This six-foot-long snake has two-inch-long fangs. A fourteen-foot cobra's fangs are one-half inch long. The reason that the Gaboon viper can have such long fangs is that it folds them back when they are not in use. The cobra's fangs are constantly erect.

Gaboon viper

The Gaboon viper makes its home in the tropical rain forests of central Africa. It is the largest of the true vipers, reaching a length of six feet. It has a wide, heavy body with a head larger than a man's fist. Its colors are like a carpet pattern of dark and light browns, yellows, and purples. The pattern makes this viper difficult to see among the leaves on the forest floor.

Despite its large teeth and very powerful venom, the Gaboon viper is not a great threat to people. Reports of bites are very rare even among the natives who walk barefooted. If the Gaboon viper is annoyed, it hisses, flattens its body, and makes short lunges at its enemy. That's enough to chase most people away. But if a person is bitten, death often quickly follows.

The Gaboon viper hunts for small rodents during the night. It uses its huge fangs and venom to kill its prey. Its strike is lightning-fast despite the slow way it usually moves around.

The *puff adder* lives all over Africa except in the rain forests. Many live in dry areas that are semideserts. The puff adder gets its name from its behavior when alarmed. It puffs itself up and hisses a warning.

The puff adder is something like a smaller edition of the Gaboon viper, with a carpet pattern of dark and light colors over its body. It grows to about five feet long, is heavy bodied, and has one-inch-long fangs. The puff adder is also a night hunter of rodents.

The puff adder is a dangerous snake. Its strike is very fast, either frontward or sideways. While its poison is slow acting, it can still cause death. Just a few years ago, the director of the Salt Lake City Zoo died from the bite of a puff adder he was handling, despite the fact that he was treated with anti-venin.

Russell's viper is the best known and most common of the vipers that live in Asia. This viper has a powerful venom and a bad disposition. It is a constant threat to the population and

is probably responsible for more deaths than the cobras.

When Arthur Conan Doyle wrote about the "speckled

band" in a Sherlock Holmes story, he was referring to Russell's viper. A grown viper is about five and a half feet long and has enough venom to kill several people. Even a small viper can inject enough venom to kill a healthy person. Its usual food is small rodents, but it will also eat frogs and lizards.

Russell's viper

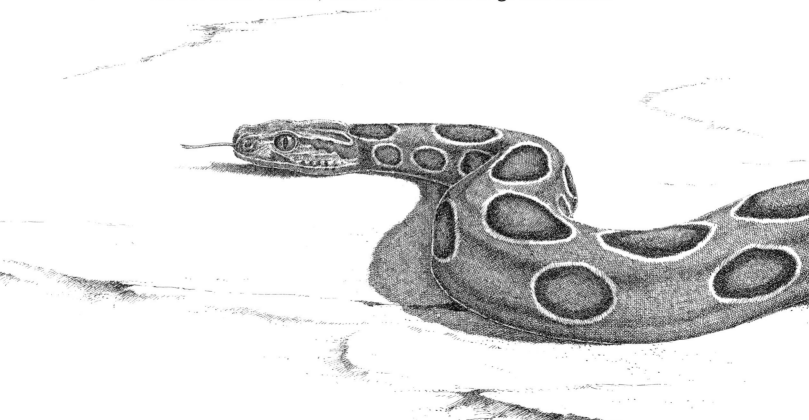

The *rhinoceros viper* is closely related to the Gaboon viper and the puff adder. Its name comes from the scales above its nostrils, which look something like a horn. It is about four feet long and has a pattern of black and blue patches down its back, with a yellow line through the center.

This viper lives in swampy areas of central Africa. It hunts for food in much the same way as its larger relatives. It has a powerful poison and is greatly feared by the natives.

The *European viper,* or *adder,* is the only poisonous snake in England and in many parts of Europe. It has a very wide range in Europe, is found far north in Scandinavia and all the way east to central Asia. It is a small snake, only about two feet long. There is a great deal of variation in their markings, but most European vipers have a dark zigzag line down their *rhinoceros viper* backs.

European vipers are not very dangerous. There are very few reported deaths due to their bites. They are unlikely to bite unless handled foolishly. They normally eat many kinds of small animals, including rodents and lizards.

The *horned vipers* and the *saw-scaled vipers* are, for their size, the most poisonous of all the vipers. Most of them are two feet long; some may reach three feet. The horned vipers move across the desert sands by a method called sidewinding. (See p. 67.) This makes them seem to roll along.

These kinds of vipers are very common in dry areas and are found from North Africa to India and Sri Lanka (Ceylon). Some kinds can also be found in parts of Europe. The vipers have a habit of lying in paths in open places on the ground.

If a person steps on them by accident, they have a lightning-fast bite that is highly poisonous. They cause many deaths in places such as Egypt or India, where people go barefooted or without thick shoes.

Pit vipers look much the same as their close relatives, the true vipers. The main difference is the depression, or "pit," between the eyes and the nostrils of all pit vipers. The pits look like a pair of second nostrils, but they have nothing to do with smelling.

Each pit is really a special organ that is sensitive to warmth. The snakes use the pits to detect warm-blooded prey: mammals and birds. Scientists have shown that pit vipers can even be blindfolded and still strike accurately at a warm object held in front of them. A person's hand, for example, can be sensed more than a foot away.

The pits help direct the snake toward its prey as well as position its strike. A blindfolded copperhead will turn in the direction of a warm object moving five or six feet in front of

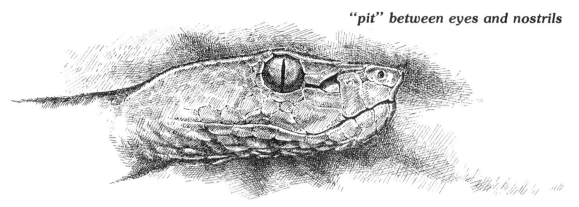

49

it. But it will not strike until the warm object comes within range. The pits are a great help for a pit viper hunting at night.

Most of the pit vipers live in North and South America, but a few kinds live in eastern Asia. Pit vipers are often larger than true vipers and equally as poisonous. None has fangs as long as the Gaboon viper's, but a pit viper's fangs are often larger than a cobra's.

The venom glands and ducts are about the same in true vipers and in pit vipers. Pit vipers have no teeth in their upper jaws except their poison fangs. As with other poisonous snakes, replacement fangs are present in bones in the roof of the mouth.

The *bushmaster* of Central and South America is the largest viper in the world—the biggest bushmasters are over twelve feet long. It is also one of the most dangerous snakes in the world. It often attacks people for no apparent reason. And its venom supply is more than enough to kill several people.

The bushmaster is the only pit viper in the Americas that lays eggs. All the other American pit vipers bear living young. In snakes, live bearing means that the eggs are kept in the body until they hatch. The bushmaster lays about one dozen eggs at a time, and in some cases may even guard them until they hatch.

There are many stories told about the bushmaster, some suggesting that it is very dangerous and others that it is rather harmless. For example, here is a description of an encounter with a bushmaster in the rain forest of the upper Amazon.

A geologist and two of his assistants were walking along a trail, carrying backpacks. Suddenly the man in the rear felt

bushmaster

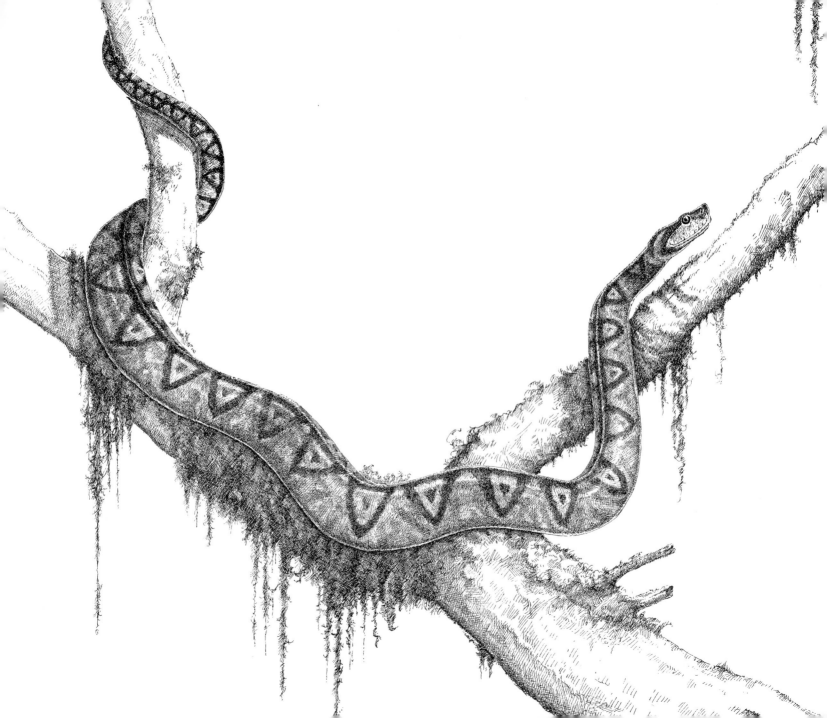

something strike his backpack. He turned around and saw a large snake thrashing around on the pack. He screamed and dropped the pack. The snake had its fangs stuck in the canvas. The men killed the snake with a machete and found it to be an *eight-foot bushmaster.* If he had not been protected by his pack, the man would likely have been killed.

One scientist studying snakes says that the bushmaster is the most dangerous snake in South America because it does not run away from people the way that other snakes do. Natives in the area say that persons bitten by bushmasters do not live long enough to reach hospitals.

On the other hand, there is this story printed in the August 1957 issue of *Copeia,* a scientific journal concerned with reptiles and fishes. The story tells of the capture of an eight-foot-long bushmaster in South America. A man and his wife were swimming in a stream when they spotted a snake. Mistaking it for a harmless kind, they decided to collect it for a scientist friend.

The amateur collectors tied a shoestring (!) around the snake's neck and started to lead the snake back home. When the snake got stubborn and refused to move, the man's wife shoved and pushed it from behind. They met an Indian who told them that the "harmless" snake was a bushmaster. Still, they picked it up and carried it back, nearly strangling the snake by accident.

So which story are we to believe: that the bushmaster is the most dangerous snake in South America, or that it just won't bite no matter how badly it is treated? The truth is that bushmasters, like all snakes, vary from one individual to another. Some are very aggressive, while others are more timid. In any event, bushmasters, like all poisonous snakes, should be avoided wherever possible.

The *fer-de-lance* is another dangerous snake that lives in tropical areas of the Americas. It is not as large as the bushmaster, only about four feet long on the average, but it is much more common. Its venom is deadly and fast acting, even more so than the bushmaster's. One scientist commented that the fer-de-lance is dangerous because it is nervous and bites readily, while the bushmaster is much calmer and will not bite as easily.

The fer-de-lance gives birth to fifty or more living young at one time. The young snakes are about ten inches long. Each of the young is able to give a poisonous bite soon after it is born.

The fer-de-lance has many close relatives that live in the tropical areas of the Americas. Some of these snakes live in trees, others on the ground. All are poisonous to a greater or lesser extent.

fer-de-lance

55

The *water moccasin,* or *cottonmouth,* is found in the southeastern United States, mainly in the swamplands of Mississippi and Florida. It is almost always found in or near swamps or slow-moving streams. As you might expect, the water moccasin eats fish, frogs, and other small animals that live in watery places.

The water moccasin rarely grows to more than five feet in length. Its body is covered with dark bands on a background of brown or muddy green. When aroused, it opens its mouth wide. The inside of its mouth is white and stands out against the dark of its body. The white mouth is the reason for the snake's nickname of "cottonmouth."

The water moccasin's poison is about as strong as that of a rattlesnake. Its bite can cause pain and death. This snake is an excellent swimmer and will usually move away from people rapidly. But there are stories where an individual snake attacked even though it could have escaped.

water moccasin or cottonmouth

The much smaller *copperhead* is not as poisonous as the water moccasin. It is found in the eastern United States from Florida and Texas in the south to New England in the north. Copperheads usually live in forested areas where there is plenty of ground cover. They feed on mice, insects, and other small animals.

The copperhead gets its name from the coppery color of its head. The rest of its body is brown with darker crossbands. Adult copperheads are usually less than a yard long. Bites from copperheads are not uncommon, but they are almost never fatal.

copperhead

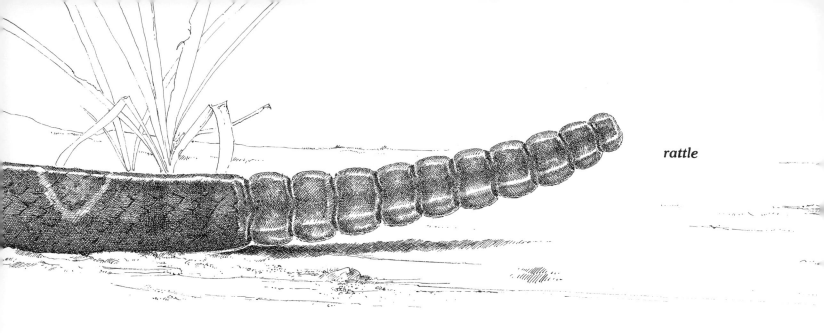

rattle

RATTLESNAKES

All rattlesnakes are pit vipers: They have the heat-sensing pits on their heads. About the only real difference between a rattler and another pit viper is the rattle at the end of its tail. However, rattlesnakes are found mainly in North America and most species are found in the United States.

The states in which bites most often occur are Arizona, Florida, Georgia, Texas, and Alabama. But rattlesnakes are found in every mainland state except Maine and Delaware (where they seem to have been exterminated). There are more different kinds of rattlers in the southwest United States and northwest Mexico than any other place. Only two kinds of rattlers are known in South America.

The rattle is made of special interlocking scales at the end of the snake's tail. A baby rattler is born with a hard little buttonlike scale at the tip of its tail. This is soon shed along with its skin. Then the first rattle appears, a bell-shaped, dry, hollow scale on the tail. Each time the skin is shed, a new rattle appears until there are about six or seven. After that, the end of the tail usually breaks off, so that only rarely will a rattler have as many as a dozen rattles.

When the tail is shaken—as fast as sixty times a second— the rattles hit against one another and make a noise. The noise doesn't really sound much like a rattle at all. Some people compare it to the sound that steam makes when it escapes from a radiator. Other people think it sounds like a buzzing insect. Yet the noise of the rattle can be very loud. A large rattlesnake can be heard one hundred feet away.

Interestingly, rattlesnakes are deaf and cannot hear their own or another snake's rattle. The rattle seems to be used to frighten enemies away. It is not used to warn the rattler's prey, since that would only make it more difficult for the snake to get food. As a warning, it is similar to the spreading of a cobra's hood or the hissing of a puff adder.

The rattle seems to be used with some animals but not with others. A rattler will not rattle its tail when approached or attacked by a king snake, for example. It simply defends itself with its fangs as well as it can. On the other hand, the sound of a rattle often prevents a weasel from coming near or a buffalo from stepping on the snake.

Rattlesnakes live in many different kinds of places, from deserts and prairies to forests and mountainous regions. Some live in rocky places, others in dense plant growth. They prey upon rabbits, prairie dogs, ground squirrels, and all kinds of small animals, including lizards and birds.

Despite their effective poison and large fangs, rattlesnakes are preyed upon by many enemies. Human beings, of course, are the rattler's greatest enemy. Many people coming upon a rattler will try to kill it. Other enemies include hawks, owls, ravens, roadrunners, coyotes, foxes, and king snakes. Some hoofed animals such as deer are known to kill rattlers by trampling on them.

The *eastern diamondback rattlesnake* is the largest poisonous snake in North America. The largest ones grow to a length of over eight feet and have fangs up to one inch long. The snake is found in coastal areas of the southeastern United States.

The eastern diamondback rattlesnake is not a very aggressive snake. It may be dangerous, however, if approached too closely. This sometimes happens because the snake often does not rattle until a person is almost upon it. This rattler is usually not found near where many people live.

The *western diamondback rattlesnake* is not quite as large as its eastern relative, but it is much more abundant. The western diamondback lives in deserts and prairies from Mississippi to California. It is a very aggressive snake, quick to rattle and ready to strike when anyone comes too near. It is said to be responsible for more serious bites and deaths than any other snake in North America. Even a young western diamondback can give a person a fatal bite.

eastern diamondback rattlesnake

The *sidewinder* lives in the deserts of the southwestern states. It has an unusual way of traveling over the loose, shifting sands. Most snakes move forward by shifting from side to side so that a series of waves passes down their bodies. But the sidewinder moves differently.

Only two points of the snake's body touch the ground, one near the front, the other near the rear. One of the points is picked up and laid down ahead of the other. This makes the snake move sideways to the direction in which the head is pointing. As the sidewinder moves, it leaves J-shaped tracks in the sand.

The sidewinder is a small rattler, usually only about one and one-half feet long. It usually hunts for its food at night and lies hidden beneath the sand during the hot day. It is sometimes called the horned rattlesnake because of a horn above each eye. The horns may stop the sand from drifting over its eyes when the sidewinder lies buried during the heat of the day.

sidewinder

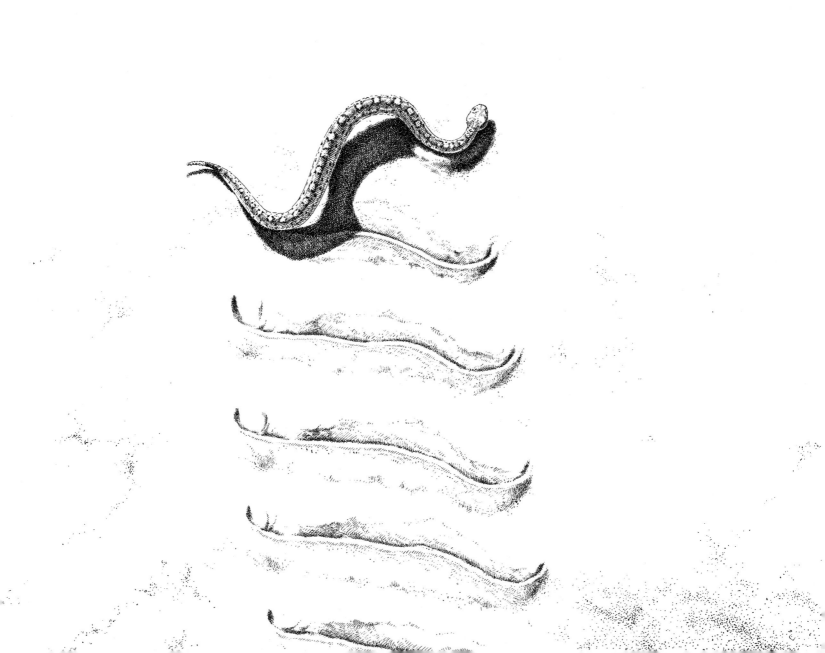

The *timber rattlesnake* is commonly found in the eastern parts of the United States. The timber rattlesnake was the first rattler encountered by the early colonists. They sent back terrible tales of its size and ferocity. The truth is that the snake is neither very large nor very aggressive. It will bite only if it is cornered and cannot escape.

The *prairie rattlesnake* is a common rattler of the western states. It rarely grows to more than four or five feet in length. It hunts for rodents during the day and is probably the rattler most often encountered by people. Both the prairie and the timber rattlesnakes are found in Canada as well as in the United States.

Two much smaller rattlesnakes found in the United States are the *massasauga* and the *pygmy rattler*. They are usually less than two feet long. Their rattles are not very developed and the sound they make is only a high-pitched buzz. They are only slightly poisonous and their bites are not fatal.

HOW DANGEROUS ARE POISONOUS SNAKES?

There is no doubt that poisonous snakes are very dangerous animals. Snakes kill more people in one year than sharks kill in one hundred years. In fact, snakes are responsible for more deaths than all the other dangerous animals in the world combined.

But for you to worry about being bitten by a poisonous snake just doesn't make sense. If you live in the United States or Canada, there is a bigger chance of being struck by lightning than of being bitten by a poisonous snake. And there is a much better chance of surviving a snakebite than a lightning bolt.

For example, the annual death toll in the United States from rattlesnake bites is about ten. The population of the United States is about 200 million. So the chance of dying from a rattlesnake bite is about one out of twenty million.

There are usually fewer than one thousand bites reported each year in the United States. Your chances of being bitten are very low. But that does not mean that rattlesnakes or other poisonous snakes are not dangerous. Any poisonous snake should be avoided and certainly never handled by an unskilled person.

Certain places in the United States *are* dangerous because of the large rattlesnake population living in the area. In these regions it would be wise to wear long trousers or tall boots. It would be foolish to walk in the woods barefooted or bare-legged. If you go walking in a remote area, it would be better if you traveled with a companion rather than going alone. Also, take along a first-aid kit with instructions for treating snakebite.

western diamondback rattlesnake

In case someone is bitten by a snake you think is poisonous, the snake should be killed and kept for identification. Even after the snake is killed it should be handled only by its tail. Medical help should be summoned as quickly as possible.

In the meantime, the patient should remain quiet and not move around. The bitten arm or leg should be left hanging down and kept still. If you know how to apply a tourniquet, it should be tight enough to cut off the blood in the veins only, not in the arteries. The tourniquet pressure must be released *every few minutes.*

If you are not knowledgeable in applying a tourniquet, don't try. An improperly applied tourniquet can harm more than help.

The object of first aid for poisonous bites is to slow down the spread of the poison until medical help arrives. In those areas that are troubled by poisonous snakes, doctors and hospitals are usually well supplied with the necessary anti-venin.

Of course, poisonous snakes that come into populated areas must be destroyed. No one wants to come into his home and find a cobra under the bed.

But it is a mistake to think of *all* poisonous snakes as enemies. Poisonous snakes play an important part in the balance of nature. In certain areas of the world, poisonous snakes kill untold millions of rodents each year. Rodents eat food crops and often spread disease.

If all the poisonous snakes were to disappear, the rodent population would increase greatly. Crops would be destroyed. Perhaps there would be more human suffering because of lack of food and the spread of disease than the snakes could ever cause.

The great dislike that some people have for snakes is remarkable. For example, some claim that snakes are slimy or dirty to the touch. Of course, they are neither. Snakes have a dry, scaly skin and are no dirtier than any other animal.

Young children rarely become afraid of snakes by themselves. The dislike of snakes is something that they learn from other people, not from seeing snakes at close hand or from handling them. The truth is that most snakes are harmless. And, overall, snakes do far more good than harm.

INDEX